Barbara & The Grocery Train Adventure

A Funny, Heartwarming Tale of Snacks, Scooters, and Saying Yes to Life

Lacey Hill-Joga & Deedra Abboud

ISBN: 978-1-956565-51-5

Lacey is a retired U.S. Army veteran who swapped combat boots for paintbrushes and a beautifully chaotic life stitched together with homeschool schedules, endless doctor's appointments, and spontaneous kitchen dance parties—courtesy of Barbara, her misbehaving left leg.

Diagnosed with Lyme disease in 2009 and multiple sclerosis soon after, Lacey now channels her creativity and resilience into art, storytelling, and homeschooling her two curious, lively daughters alongside her husband George—a Navy man with Army roots.

The Barbara Chronicles is Lacey's children's book series chronicling her funny, heartfelt journey through MS—with one rebellious leg and a few other uncooperative roommates.

Follow Lacey's journey—one story, one smile, one step at a time.

In the land of Lanie-Lou, nestled
between Laundry Mountain and the
Great Couch Plains,
there lived a peculiar
stowaway named Barbara.

She wasn't a dragon, or a wizard, or
even a mischievous gnome—
she was Lainie's very own wobbling,
wiggling, rebellious left leg.

Barbara clung to Lainie
like a stack of grumpy pancakes,
heavy as a sleepy walrus in a tutu,
and just as unpredictable.
A true diva.

And Barbara was always tired.
But when Barbara got tired, she didn't
lie down and nap—oh no.
She dragged Lainie down into the
depths of the Drowsy Seas with her.

Walking more than five minutes?
HA! That was a Barbara Joke.

One sunny day, while Ramon the Brave
was off battling dragons aboard a
mighty naval ship, Lainie faced
a dire quest of her own:
the pantry was plundered.

No peanut butter.
No cereal.
Not even a square of
toilet treasure paper.

The fridge echoed like a haunted cave.

Something had to be done.

Unfortunately, Barbara had already declared it a full-on "Nope Day."

Lainie eyed the garage.
That's when she saw it—her noble red scooter, gleaming like a knight's steed awaiting battle.

And next to it, the kids' bright yellow wagon, perfect for hauling treasure—or two pint-sized pirates.

"Barbara," Lainie whispered, steadying herself. "You may be wobbly, but we're off to claim the bounty."

She tied the wagon to the scooter with an ancient bungee cord (possibly enchanted), tossed her purse into the basket, and pointed dramatically toward the horizon.

"ALL ABOARD THE GROCERY TRAIN!"

Bina (five) and Gigi (seven) clambered
aboard with squeals of glee,
gripping the wagon rails
like seasoned deckhands.

Off they sailed—vroom-vroom!—through
the streets of the naval base and
across Sidewalk Strait.
People waved.
Birds tweeted.
One squirrel nearly fainted
from excitement.

The Grocery Train—red scooter in front, yellow caboose behind—rolled up to the marketplace like royalty.

Lanie, Barbara, and her loyal crew glided through the sliding glass gates of destiny.

Without dismounting, Lanie piloted the vessel straight into the checkout cove. "Unload the cargo, my crew!"

Bina and Gigi sprang into action like nimble pirates on a raid.

They stacked cereal, fruit snacks, and beef sticks onto the conveyor plank.

Lanie paid the gold.

The cashier gave a knowing salute.

The bagboy followed, repacking their booty into the wagon like a good ship's quartermaster.

Bagged groceries piled between their
knees, juice boxes poking elbows,
the girls grinned as they
sailed homeward in triumph.

Barbara, soothed by the wind and the
wheels, behaved herself.

From that day forth,
the Grocery Train was legend.

It didn't just visit the marketplace—
it voyaged to the post office,
cruised through the library lagoon, and
even explored the wild wooded trails
beyond Laundry Mountain.

It beeped its horn at wayward beasts.
It waved at butterflies
like visiting nobility.

Barbara, when she got to ride instead of
march, was much less mutinous.

But not every voyage was smooth sailing.

One crisp afternoon, while gliding down a leafy trail with the wind in their sails and adventure in their hearts—CRACK!

The wagon struck a knobbly root.

A big one.

The caboose flipped like an overturned treasure chest.

Lainie screeched to a halt, eyes wide with horror and hilarity.

Kids? Overboard.
Apples? Rolling down the hill.
Lanie? Laughing so hard
she nearly lost the helm.

"Barbara!" she gasped, bracing herself on
the handlebars. "You couldn't have
warned me about the sea monster?"

Barbara, naturally, said nothing.
Just a twitch in Lanie's side and a tug in
her left leg that meant,
"Let's not do that again."

Bina and Gigi? Completely unharmed
and wildly delighted.

After brushing off leaves and retrieving scattered treasures, the Grocery Train was back on track—because in Lanie-Lou, even a tip-over was just part of the adventure.

So yes, Barbara still made things tricky—slow, wobbly, occasionally dramatic—but Lainie found ways to carry her anyway.

With a scooter,
a wagon,
two brave daughters, and
an excellent sense of humor,
no quest was truly impossible.

Not with the Grocery Train.

Choo-choo, and onward!

If you *enjoyed* this book, we'd be so *grateful* if you'd share the *love* by leaving a *review* on Amazon!

★ ★ ★ ★ ★

More from the "Barbara Chronicles" Series:

Whoa There, Barbara!

(Coming Soon) *Oh, Barbara... Get It Together!*
(Coming soon) *Barbara & the Couch Kingdom*
(Coming soon) *Barbara & the Midnight Snack Heist*
(Coming soon) *Barbara & the Dragon at Laundry Mountain*